Since 1888, *National Geographic* magazine has provided its readers a wealth of information and helped us understand the world in which we live. Insightful articles, supported by gorgeous photography and impeccable research, bring the mission of the National Geographic Society front and center: to inspire people to care about the planet. The *Explore* series delivers National Geographic to you in the same spirit. Each of the books in this series presents the best articles on popular and relevant topics in an accessible format. In addition, each book highlights the work of National Geographic explorers, photographers, and writers. Explore the world of *National Geographic.* You will be inspired.

ON THE COVER
Aerial of the Giza Pyramids next to modern city of Cairo

What's the first image that leaps to mind when you think about ancient Egypt? Odds are it's either a mummy or a pyramid. Mummies are preserved human remains, and the pyramids are monumental tombs for some of Egypt's pharaohs, or rulers. With these images in mind, it's easy to think of ancient Egypt as a dead civilization.

The people living in Egypt thousands of years ago certainly did not think of their world as a dead place. They lived in a rich and complex society. Farmers followed the rhythm of the river Nile's floods to bring forth their harvests. The government collected taxes. Architects designed massive temples, which were then built by workers and craftsmen. People from all walks of life worked, studied, played, and loved—just like you do today.

In ancient times, the Egyptians believed that burying their dead in a certain way would ensure that their souls would survive in the afterlife. For that reason, people were buried with items their families believed they could use in the afterlife. What's found in tombs is a source of information not just about death but also about life in ancient Egypt. The items represent the things people valued and used every day. The mummies themselves have revealed information about the health, lifestyles, and diet of the ancient Egyptians.

The articles in this collection have been adapted from National Geographic publications. They will help you explore several aspects of life and death in ancient Egypt. You will learn why pharaohs built their tombs in the shape of pyramids, and you will meet two of the most intriguing pharaohs. You will also find insights into the lives of everyday Egyptians. Like people you know, they worried about their looks, kept beloved pets, and worked to earn a living. From today's perspective, you will read about technology that is bringing to light new facts about ancient lives.

As you read, we hope you will gain a greater understanding of those famous mummies and pyramids and also of the people who created them.

TREASURED PETS
Animal mummies were common in ancient Egypt, and cats were particularly valued.

DAWN OF THE
Pyramids

The first kings of the Nile Valley began a new era of burial customs. They started with simple, underground graves. As time went on, they made more complex preparations for life in the next world. These led to ancient Egypt's best-known monuments—the majestic Pyramids of Giza.

BY A. R. WILLIAMS

Adapted from "Dawn of the Pyramids," by A. R. Williams,
from National Geographic *Exploring History*, Fall 2011

FIRST PYRAMID
Pharaoh Djoser's Step Pyramid at Saqqara was once the largest building of its time.

The Pyramids of Giza are not the only great buildings that hold the secrets of ancient Egypt. Just 300 miles to the south of this giant burial ground are tombs from an earlier time. They are less famous but just as important. They were built at a time when Egypt was young, and they harbor clues to that important period.

A thousand years before pyramids began to rise at Giza, the country's rulers were experimenting with ideas they hoped would make them as powerful in death as they were in life. Their ideas would inspire King Khufu, who built the Great Pyramid at Giza in 2550 B.C. They continued to influence **elite** Egyptian burials for the next 3,000 years.

In an earlier period in Egypt's history, there were no kings. Rather, a patchwork of chiefdoms, each with its own gods and government, spread along the Nile. They reached from the Sudan in the far south to the Mediterranean coast in the north. As local leaders fought for control, strong rulers arose in southern Egypt. The date was around 3100 B.C.

Then along came the first king. His name may have been Menes, or Narmer, or both—experts aren't sure. This man from the south was finally able to unify all groups into one mighty civilization. He founded the first of Egypt's 30 **dynasties**.

The site known as Abydos was the king's capital city. There, archaeologists have found burials that reveal distinctive post-death practices. The burials were designed to show off the rulers' newly gained power.

UNIFYING EGYPT
This decorated stone shows the legendary first ruler of a unified Egypt subduing a conquered enemy.

The First Tombs

By the time the early kings began to plan their tombs, some traditions had already taken hold. For example, the dead were laid to rest parallel to the course of the Nile, which runs south to north.

Since the beginning of life along the Nile, people had buried their dead in the desert to save the fertile land along the river for farming. A grave was usually a shallow hole with a mound of sand shoveled over the body. Burials often included useful goods such as ceramic pots and combs of ivory and bone. These items attracted thieves. Scrabbling through the sand, the raiders took what they wanted and fled, leaving the corpse uncovered. The robberies revealed a surprising fact: Hot, dry sand absorbed the fluids produced by a body as it decayed, creating a mummy with perfectly preserved features. To the ancient Egyptians, this could only mean that a body stayed intact after death by being buried under a hill.

That idea reinforced the **mystical** aspect of Egypt's central yearly event, the flooding of the Nile. Every year, the floods fertilized fields and brought forth an abundance of food. As the river retreated to normal levels after months of high water, the first lands to reappear were hilltops. Within hours, life returned in shades of green. That yearly miracle gave rise to the myth of the first hill emerging from watery **chaos**. To the ancient Egyptians, that first hill was Atum, the god who created the world. Based on those observations and beliefs, each early ruler included a model of the first hill in the design of his tomb. As a symbol of creation and rebirth, the hill was intended to help him fulfill his kingly destiny—being reborn in the next life.

3200–3065 B.C.
Early Egyptian graves were simple holes in the sand. Before the 1st dynasty, royal burials became more sophisticated, with underground chambers and rich funerary offerings.

3065–2890 B.C.
Kings of the 1st dynasty were buried at Abydos. Each ruler had an underground tomb. The funerary complex also included a structure aboveground.

2890–2686 B.C.
Early kings of the 2nd dynasty were buried at Saqqara, part of the great cemetery near Memphis. Their tombs were also underground; no traces of aboveground structures have survived.

2686–2613 B.C.
At the beginning of the 3rd dynasty, King Djoser officially moved the royal cemetery from Abydos to Saqqara. His newly designed funerary complex included Egypt's first pyramid.

Tombs in the 1st dynasty didn't soar like the pyramids. However, they did launch a new, complex burial style. A central chamber was surrounded by several rooms for offerings. The entire tomb was covered by a wooden roof. Above the roof stood a re-creation of the first hill. Essentially a pyramid in the making, it was a mound of sand and rubble that sloped in four directions to reach the tomb's rectangular edge. The mound was enclosed by a wall. Oddly, all these features were underground, so the symbolism was hidden.

As a royal tomb was created, a **compound** known as a **funerary** palace was built about half a mile away. This was a chapel set in a two-acre courtyard surrounded by mud-brick walls several feet thick and more than 30 feet tall. The main gate opened in the southeast corner. This detail would show up three centuries later in a new type of tomb.

The funerary palace was an imposing structure and must have had a symbolic role, but experts still don't know what it was. To add to the mystery, each compound was torn down shortly after it was completed.

All these early burials and funerary structures were built in a dry riverbed. The wide ravine ran from the Nile's lush floodplain in the east to a gap in the rocky cliffs in the west. The ancient Egyptians believed this gap was the gateway to the afterworld.

A New Royal Cemetery

For a time during the 2nd dynasty, royal burials shifted to Saqqara, part of the cemetery for the city of Memphis. Memphis sat just south of the Nile's delta, where the river narrowed a great deal. Whoever held that checkpoint controlled access to the whole country and gained a major military and political edge. Eventually, Memphis became the capital of Egypt.

The 2nd-dynasty royal tombs at Saqqara kept all the underground elements of the Abydos tombs, but they were arranged in a straight line. The burial chamber lay at the end of a corridor flanked by offering rooms. Some experts have suggested that a funerary palace may have stood directly above this, but none has survived.

At the end of the 2nd dynasty, a ruler named Djoser took the throne, launching a new dynasty along with an era of **innovation**. For starters, Djoser officially established the royal cemetery at Saqqara, where it remained for the next 450 years.

DIVINE POWER
Two goddesses flank an image of King Menkaure. The king's idealized features testify to the godlike status of ancient Egypt's rulers.

7

A NOBLE TOMB
The basic layout of this 6th dynasty tomb is a burial shaft covered by a richly decorated building. This layout may have influenced the design of royal burials.

As he began to prepare his final resting place there, he would alter the shape of the royal tomb quite magnificently.

Djoser originally planned to be buried as earlier kings were: under a square-sided artificial hill set within a wall. Then he changed his mind.

Invention of the Pyramid

After expanding it twice, Djoser decided his tomb needed a more impressive profile. Around 2650 B.C. he began to build upward, creating a stack of four tiers. Each tier was smaller than the one beneath it. It seems that wasn't monumental enough, so he added two more. The resulting structure, almost 200 feet tall, was the world's first stone pyramid. Known today as the Step Pyramid of Saqqara, it functioned as a stairway to the heavens for the dead king.

To enhance the pyramid's setting, Djoser kept with tradition and had a wall built around it. The structure was massive, with a gate set in the southeastern corner, just like the walls of the funerary palaces at Abydos. Also, Djoser oriented the compound south to north, like the early burials.

While he reigned over Egypt, Djoser—like other kings—had to perform an important state **ritual** called the Heb Sed. Through this ceremony, the king restored his **vitality** so he could continue to maintain the maat, the cosmic order of the Nile Valley. A king was supposed to repeat the Heb Sed, even after death, for the good of his people. In preparation, Djoser re-created the Heb Sed arena inside his funerary compound, complete with models of the necessary buildings.

Changes over the next few generations would transform the new tomb design into the awe-inspiring Pyramids of Giza. This classic symbol of the first burial mounds would mark many royal tombs until the end of dynastic history. Even **King Tut** and his relatives recalled the first hill more than a thousand years after Djoser's tomb took shape. Their own burials were carved deep into limestone cliffs to hide them from thieves. Still, the beautifully painted chambers lie in the shadow of a low peak that rises skyward in the rough shape of a pyramid.

THINK ABOUT IT! |||||||||||||||||||||||||||||||||||

1 **Sequence Events** List the main events in the development of burial customs from the earliest kings to the time of King Tut.

2 **Make Inferences** How did the kings use their tombs to help show their power and importance to the people of Egypt?

3 **Distinguish Fact and Opinion** Reread the statement at the end of paragraph 2 under "The First Tombs": "To the ancient Egyptians, this could only mean that a body stayed intact after death by being buried under a hill." Is this a fact or the writer's opinion? Explain your answer.

BACKGROUND & VOCABULARY

chaos *n.* (KAY-aws) a state of total disorganization

compound *n.* (KAHM-pownd) a group of buildings

dynasty *n.* (DY-nuh-stee) a series of rulers from the same family

elite *adj.* (ay-LEET) from a high or powerful group in a society

funerary *adj.* (FYOO-nuh-ray-ree) having to do with burial and funeral practices

innovation *n.* (in-uh-VAY-shuhn) the creation of new ideas and inventions

mystical *adj.* (MIS-tuh-kuhl) having a spiritual or religious meaning

ritual *n.* (RIH-choo-uhl) religious or spiritual ceremony that is performed at specific times

vitality *n.* (vy-TAL-uh-tee) life energy

King Tut This common nickname was given to the pharaoh Tutankhamun, who reigned from 1332 to 1322 B.C. He is famous today because his tomb was one of the most complete burials ever discovered. Precious objects from King Tut's tomb have been displayed and admired on exhibit in many parts of the world. Read more about King Tut starting on page 16 in this book.

THE King HERSELF

BY CHIP BROWN

Adapted from "The King Herself," by Chip Brown, in *National Geographic*, April 2009

GODDESS QUEEN
This statue discovered in the queen's temple at Deir el Bahri portrays Hatshepsut in the form of the goddess Osiris.

Hatshepsut was one of the most accomplished rulers of ancient Egypt. During her reign she built magnificent monuments and temples. She was also a skilled politician. She is most famous, though, for her astonishing choice to rule as a king, not a queen. Follow National Geographic writer Chris Brown as he discovers the secrets of Hatshepsut.

Hatshepsut Today

I leaned toward the open display case in Cairo's Egyptian Museum and gazed at what in all likelihood is the body of Hatshepsut (hat-SHEP-soot), the extraordinary woman who ruled Egypt from 1479 to 1458 B.C. There was something touching about her fingertips, but everywhere else all human grace was gone. The ragged linen around her neck looked like a fashion statement gone wrong. Her mouth, with the upper lip shelved over the lower, was gruesome. Her eye sockets were packed with black **resin**. Her nostrils were plugged with tight rolls of cloth. Her left ear had sunk into the flesh on the side of her skull, and her head was almost bald. It was hard to connect this thing with the great ruler who lived so long ago and of whom it was written, "To look upon her was more beautiful than anything."

The discovery of Hatshepsut's lost mummy made headlines in the summer of 2007, but the full story unfolded slowly, over more than a hundred years. When they began their search, archaeologists were using brushes and small digging tools. When the search ended, their toolbox included **CT scanners** and sophisticated analysis through genetic testing. Even with all these high-tech methods, had it not been for the accidental discovery of a tooth, Hatshepsut might still be lying alone and in the dark. Instead she is enshrined in one of the two Royal Mummy Rooms at the Egyptian Museum. Plaques in Arabic and English proclaim her to be Hatshepsut, the King Herself.

Her Story

Hatshepsut's father, Thutmose (tut-MOH-suh), had been a powerful general who married into the royal family. Her mother was a true royal princess, descended from the pharaohs. When Thutmose died, his son by another wife inherited the crown as Thutmose II. In the tradition of the time, the young king married his half sister Hatshepsut. As his wife, she became queen of Egypt.

Thutmose II did not rule for long before heart disease ushered him into the afterlife. Because his heir, Thutmose III, was still a young boy, Hatshepsut, the boy's stepmother, assumed control as the young pharaoh's queen **regent**. So began one of the most intriguing periods of ancient Egyptian history.

At first, Hatshepsut was careful to respect tradition and act on her stepson's behalf. But before long, there were signs that Hatshepsut's regency would be different. After just a few years she had assumed the role of "king" of Egypt, supreme power in the land. By then, her stepson may have been fully ready to assume the throne, but he stayed second-in-command. Hatshepsut proceeded to rule for a total of 21 years.

Hatshepsut turned out to be one of the greatest builders in one of the greatest Egyptian dynasties. She raised temples and shrines from north to south. The four granite **obelisks** she erected at **Karnak** were among the most magnificent ever constructed. She longed to be remembered and honored for all time. On one of her obelisks at

Karnak she had inscribed: "Now my heart turns this way and that, as I think what the people will say. Those who see my monuments in years to come, and who shall speak of what I have done."

Why did Hatshepsut break so completely with the traditional role of queen regent? Something drove Hatshepsut to change how she portrayed herself. No one knows why for sure.

In ancient Egypt, whether you were male or female was no small matter. The kingship was meant to be passed down from father to son, not daughter. Egyptian religious beliefs taught that the king's role could not be adequately carried out by a woman. Getting over this hurdle must have taken great shrewdness from the female king.

Hatshepsut never made a secret of being a woman. But in the early years, she seemed to be looking for ways to bring together the images of queen and king. In one statue, she is shown with the body of a woman but with a striped headdress and cobra, symbols of a king. In some temple carvings, she is dressed in a traditional ankle-length gown but standing with her feet wide apart like a king. As the years went on, she had herself shown only as a male king, without any female traits.

After Hatshepsut's death around 1458 B.C. her stepson went on to become one of Egypt's great pharaohs. Thutmose III was a monument maker like his stepmother and a fierce warrior. In the later part of his life, Thutmose III appears to have decided to wipe his stepmother, the king, out of history. He had her monuments attacked and her kingly name erased from public memorials. At Karnak her image and **cartouche**, or name symbol, were chiseled off shrine walls. Her statues were smashed and thrown into a pit in front of her burial temple.

Images of Hatshepsut as queen were not disturbed. But wherever she was pictured as king, the workers of her stepson came with their chisels, the vandalism careful and precise. According to one archaeologist, "It was a political decision." Thutmose III needed to strengthen his own son's claim to the throne in the face of rival claims from other family members. The banishment of King Hatshepsut might have served this purpose well.

"Now my heart turns this way and that, as I think what the people will say. Those who see my monuments in years to come, and who shall speak of what I have done."

Hatshepsut's Mummy

For centuries, no one knew where Hatshepsut's mummy was or whether it had even survived the destruction ordered by Thutmose III.

In the early 1900s the famous archaeologist Howard Carter found two female mummies in a minor tomb in the Valley of the Kings. One mummy was in a coffin. The other lay on the floor. She had no coffin, no headdress, no jewelry, no gold sandals or gold toe and finger coverings.

Nothing connected her with royalty. Three years later another archaeologist removed the mummy in the coffin to the Egyptian Museum. The mummy on the floor was left as she was.

Over the years Egyptologists lost track of the entrance to the tomb. The mummy on the tomb floor effectively disappeared. That changed in June 1989 when Donald Ryan, an American Egyptologist, came to explore several small, undecorated tombs in the valley. Along with another Egyptologist, he suspected that the lost tomb might house Hatshepsut's mummy. Arriving too late on his first day to start work, Ryan decided to walk around the site to drop off some tools. Carefully sweeping the area, he found a crack in the rock corridor and a set of stairs. He and a local inspector entered the lost tomb.

"It was spooky," Ryan recalls, "I had never found a mummy before. . . . I walked in very carefully. There was a woman lying on the floor. Oh my gosh!" He couldn't believe what he saw.

FACE OF A QUEEN
Though it is more than 3,500 years old, Hatshepsut's mummy is remarkably well preserved.

The mummy was lying in a tomb that had been trashed by robbers. Her left arm was crooked across her chest in a burial pose. Ryan set about cataloging what he found.

The more Ryan studied the mummy, the more he thought she might be someone important. "She was extraordinarily well mummified," he says. "And she was striking a royal pose. I thought, Why, she's a queen! Could it be Hatshepsut? Possibly. But there was nothing to link the mummy to any specific individual."

Still, it didn't seem right to leave whoever she was lying on the floor in a mess of rags. Before he closed the tomb, Ryan and a coworker tidied the chamber and put the unknown lady into a simple coffin.

Nearly 20 years later, Zahi Hawass, head of the Egyptian Mummy Project, asked the Egyptian Museum to round up all the unidentified royal female mummies. These included the body still in the tomb. Over a four-month period, the mummies passed through a CT scanner. The archaeologists examined each in detail to learn her age and cause of death. The CT results failed to connect one of the mummies with Hatshepsut.

Then Hawass had another idea. In the 19th century archaeologists had found a wooden box engraved with Hatshepsut's cartouche. In the box was a liver, thought to be hers. When the box was run through the scanner, researchers were astonished to detect a tooth. The team dentist identified it as a back tooth with part of its root missing. In the jaw of one of the mummies—the mummy from the floor of the tomb—was a root with no tooth.

Was this mummy the long-lost Hatshepsut? Scientists cannot be completely certain. They were certain enough, though, to display her among the great pharaohs. There she lies in a Royal Mummy Room, lifeless and still mysterious.

THINK ABOUT IT! ||||||||||||

1 **Form and Support Opinions** Based on what you've read, what do you think were Hatshepsut's most positive qualities? What do you think were her most negative qualities? Give your reasons.

2 **Draw Conclusions** Historians draw conclusions from the facts they learn about a historical figure. Identify one conclusion in each section of the article. Then name a fact that supports that conclusion.

3 **Synthesize** Explain this statement: Hard work, technology, and luck all had a part in discovering Hatshepsut's mummy. Include at least two details from the reading in your explanation.

BACKGROUND & VOCABULARY

cartouche *n.* (KAR-toosh) an oval figure containing the name of a ruler or god in ancient Egyptian writing

CT scanner *n.* sometimes called a "cat scanner"; medical device used to view internal human or animal tissues

Karnak (KAR-nak) This village in southern Egypt on the Nile River is the site of various temples and other buildings. Over centuries, many rulers of ancient Egypt built temples or other additions to Karnak.

obelisk *n.* (AH-buh-lisk) a tall, four-sided stone pillar

regent *n.* (REE-jehnt) one who acts in place of a king or ruler, for example when that person is too young to rule

resin *n.* (REH-zin) a sticky substance produced by some plants and trees

NileStyle

Makeup was on the minds of Egyptians, alive or dead. Burial objects included cosmetic spoons, tubes to store eyeliner, and jars for creams.

Egyptian eyes are back in fashion, with movie stars lining their lids in the style of Cleopatra. Then, as now, the desired effect was to make the eyes pop. In ancient Egypt, though, improving one's looks had spiritual aspects as well. A luxurious wig stiffened with wax, for example, linked the wearer to Hathor, goddess of beauty. Green eye paint may have been used to seek Hathor's protection.

In death, makeup created the young look considered necessary for the afterlife. Used by both men and women, makeup may also have had earthly benefits. Black eyeliner—known as kohl—was believed to keep away flies and cut the sun's glare. It also acted as a disinfectant. (Although the eyeliner contained lead, we have no evidence of any toxic results.)

For the living, oils and creams kept skin moist in the dry climate. These were often scented. Some creams were even given as wages. There were also many wrinkle remedies. Like the remedies of today, they may or may not have been effective.

ANCIENT GLAMOUR
Ancient Egyptians used kohl to outline, highlight, and protect their eyes.

THINK ABOUT IT! ||||||||||||||||||

Compare and Contrast Why did ancient Egyptians wear makeup? Why do people today wear makeup? List the similarities and differences in the reasons.

Technology & Tut

BY A. R. WILLIAMS

Adapted from "King Tut Revealed,"
by A. R. Williams, in *National Geographic*, June 2005

He was just a teenager when he died, the last heir of a powerful family that had ruled Egypt and its empire for centuries. He was laid to rest in a tomb filled with gold and eventually forgotten. Since the discovery of his tomb in 1922, the modern world has speculated about what happened to him, with murder the most extreme possibility. Leaving his tomb for the first time in almost 80 years, Tutankhamun (tut-ahn-KAH-muhn)—King Tut as he is widely known today—has undergone a CT scan that offers new clues about his life and death. The scan also provides precise data for an accurate reconstruction of the boyish pharaoh.

WHAT KILLED KING TUT?

In 2005, King Tut's mummy still rested in the plain wooden box where British archaeologist Howard Carter had placed him decades before. But scientists had a new way to examine the young pharaoh's remains. Diagnostic imaging could now be done with computed tomography, or CT. In this process, hundreds of x-rays in cross section are put together like slices of bread. The result is a three-dimensional picture of a body.

King Tut was one of the first mummies to be put through a CT scanner. Scientists scanned him head to toe, creating a total of 1,700 digital images. After recording Tut's entire body, a team of specialists in **radiology**, **forensics**, and **anatomy** began to probe the secrets protected for so long.

BURIAL TREASURES
Left: A golden shrine that held statues of Tut and his wife was found in Tut's tomb. A detail of the carving on a shrine panel shows the couple.
Top: This pendant symbolized Tut's throne. It features a scarab, a type of beetle, considered sacred to ancient Egyptians.

TUT'S TOMB

It was 6 p.m. on January 5, 2005. An angry wind stirred up ghostly dust as King Tut was taken from his resting place in the ancient Egyptian cemetery known as the Valley of the Kings. Dark clouds had scudded across the desert sky all day. Now they covered the stars in a gray veil. In a few moments the world's most famous mummy would glide headfirst into a CT scanner. Scientists were about to probe the medical mysteries of this little understood young ruler who died more than 3,300 years ago.

All afternoon the usual line of tourists from around the world had descended into the cramped tomb some 26 feet underground. They gazed at the figures on the walls of the burial chamber. They peered at Tut's **gilded** face on his mummy-shaped outer coffin lid. Some visitors read from guidebooks in a whisper. Others stood silently. Perhaps they wondered if the pharaoh's curse—death or misfortune falling upon those who disturbed him—was really true.

When the valley closed to the public at dusk, Egyptologists in jeans and laborers in long robes and turbans got to work. Shouting directions over the roar of fresh air being pumped into the tomb, they quickly attached ropes to the head and foot of the coffin lid. They lifted it out of the **sarcophagus**. After a pause to adjust the ropes, they slowly pulled up a plain wooden box. Inside were the mortal remains of King Tutankhamun: a serene face with a scarred left cheek, a barrel chest, skeletal arms and legs. The body was blackened by **resins** that were poured on during his burial rites.

"The mummy is in very bad condition because of what Carter did in the 1920s," said Zahi Hawass, secretary general of Egypt's Supreme Council of Antiquities, as he leaned over the body for a long first look.

Howard Carter discovered Tut's tomb in 1922 after years of searching. Though some of the outer rooms had been looted in ancient times, the contents of the burial itself were untouched. Its layered treasures included four nested boxes, or shrines, of gilded wood. Nested within the smallest shrine were three mummy-shaped coffins, two gilded and one of solid gold. At the

A RICH DISCOVERY
Here, in 1922, Carter peers into the inner golden shrine that held Tut's sarcophagus, his three coffins, and his mummy.

center was Tut himself, with a stunning mask of gold covering his head and shoulders.

Carter spent months carefully recording the pharaoh's burial treasures. He then began investigating the three nested coffins. Opening the first, he found a burial cloth decorated with willow and olive leaves, wild celery, lotus petals, and cornflowers. All suggested a burial in March or April. When Carter finally reached the mummy, though, he ran into trouble. The ritual resins had hardened, cementing Tut to the bottom of his solid gold coffin. "No amount of . . . force could move them," Carter wrote later. "What was to be done?"

A NEW APPROACH
A little more than 80 years after Carter discovered Tut's tomb, Egyptologist Zahi Hawass and an all-Egyptian research team remove the coffin from its resting place in order to scan the remains inside.

The sun can beat down like a hammer this far south in Egypt. Carter tried to use the sun's heat to loosen the resins. For several hours he set the mummy outside in blazing sunshine that heated it to 149 degrees. Nothing budged. He reported calmly that "the [hardened] material had to be chiseled away from beneath the [body] . . . before it was possible to raise the king's remains."

In his defense, Carter really had little choice. If he hadn't cut the mummy free, thieves most certainly would have broken into the tomb and ripped it apart to remove the gold. In Tut's time the royals were fabulously wealthy, and they thought—or hoped—they could take their riches with them in the afterlife.

For his journey to the great beyond, King Tut was lavished with glittering goods: precious collars, necklaces, bracelets, rings, a ceremonial apron, sandals, coverings for his fingers and toes, and the inner coffin and mask—all of pure gold. To separate Tut from his adornments, Carter's men removed the mummy's head and cut apart nearly every major joint. Once they had finished, they reassembled the remains on a layer of sand in a wooden box.

The treasures found in King Tut's tomb make up the richest royal collection ever found. They have become part of the pharaoh's legend. The striking artifacts in gold caused a sensation at the time of Carter's discovery. They still get the most attention. But Tut was also buried with everyday things he'd want in the afterlife: board games, a bronze razor, linen undergarments, cases of food and wine. Archaeologists today focus more on these types of items, with their fascinating glimpses into daily life and ancient beliefs about the afterlife.

CLUES FROM TOP . . .

Did the young pharaoh die from a blow to the head? Definitely not, say the nine doctors who studied the CT images. Some Egyptologists have long speculated that a murderer attacked Tut from behind. As evidence, they cite an x-ray taken in 1968. It shows a piece of bone in the skull cavity, which had been emptied by **embalmers**, according to custom. The CT scan, however, found no trace of a deadly blow to the head. The scan did reveal two loose pieces of bone, as well as additional chips in the embalming resins that line the top and back of the skull. Packing material also appears near the ears and in the sinus cavities, and plugs close the nostrils. To remove the brain, pour in the resins, and stuff in the packing, the embalmers likely entered the skull through the nose and the neck, perhaps breaking off bone in the process. Carter's handling of the mummy may also have produced bone chips.

The maturity of the skeleton and wisdom teeth confirms that Tut was about 19 years old when he died. Typical of a young person, his teeth had no cavities. The elongated shape of his skull was similar to that of other family members. It was not caused by disease as some had thought.

. . . TO BOTTOM

About five feet six inches tall and slightly built, Tut was in excellent health. He was well fed and free of any disease that would have affected his physical development. Though his spine appears curved, it was probably positioned that way during embalming. Something out of the ordinary, then, must have struck him down. But what? The experts can't say for sure because of the difficulty in separating possible injuries to Tut while alive and the damage Carter's team did to the mummy. Some believe, for instance, that

a fracture above the left knee was Carter's fault. Others think it may be the result of an accident or attack. An infection might have set in at the site of the break and spread, causing his death.

Could King Tut have died quickly from an illness? Letters from the time reveal that a plague was ravaging Egypt and its neighbors. Plague could have killed Tut, but no physical evidence points to that cause.

Could he have died in battle or crashed his chariot while hunting? Items buried in his tomb—including chariots, bows, arrows, and throwing sticks—indicate that he had learned to hunt and fight like a proper pharaoh. It's easy to imagine him at the reigns of a chariot feeling a young man's need for speed. He hits a bump, flies through the air, and lands with a deadly crunch. Supporters of this possibility point to Tut's chest. Its breastbone is missing, and much of the front rib cage is cut out. Did the embalmers take them out because they were already badly damaged? It's an interesting question, but for now the pharaoh is still keeping some secrets.

THE SCAN OF TUT'S BODY

The night of the CT scan, workmen carried Tut from the tomb in his box. They climbed a ramp and a flight of stairs into the swirling sand outside. Then workmen and mummy were mechanically raised into the trailer that held the scanner. Twenty minutes later two men emerged, ran to an office nearby, and returned with a pair of white plastic fans. The million-dollar scanner had quit because of sand in a cooler fan. "Curse of the pharaoh," joked a guard nervously.

Eventually the new fans worked well enough to finish the procedure. After checking that no data had been lost, the **technicians** turned Tut over to the workmen. They carried him back to his tomb. Less than three hours after he was removed from his coffin, the pharaoh again rested in peace where priests had laid him so long ago.

Back in the trailer a technician pulled up astonishing images of Tut on a computer screen. A gray head took shape, and the technician spun and tilted it in every direction. Neck bones appeared. Other images revealed a hand, several views of the rib cage, and a section of the skull.

Treasures from Tut's Tomb

LEATHER SANDALS >
The designs on these sandals depict traditional enemies of Egypt. Walking in the sandals, Tut symbolically stepped on Egypt's foes.

IVORY HEADREST ⌄
This ritual headrest was one of four found in Tut's tomb. Here, two lions flank Shu, the god of the air, who holds the sky on his shoulders.

GOLDEN THRONE ⌃
Discovered in a pile of furniture in the tomb, Tut's throne is made of wood, gold leaf, silver, and semi-precious stones. Lions, winged serpents, and hooded cobras protected the king as he sat on this spectacular throne.

BOARD GAME ⌄
Carved from a single piece of ivory, this board game was one of several buried with Tut. Royal tombs were ritually packed with food, trinkets, and other items that might be needed in the afterlife.

Burying Tut

Laying Tut to rest was like packing a present within a present. Tut's mummy, covered in wrappings and his gold funeral mask, was placed in the inner coffin. Two larger coffins held the inner coffin. The coffins were then nested in a beautifully carved stone sarcophagus. Finally, four gilded, or gold-covered, shrines were built one after the other to enclose the sarcophagus.

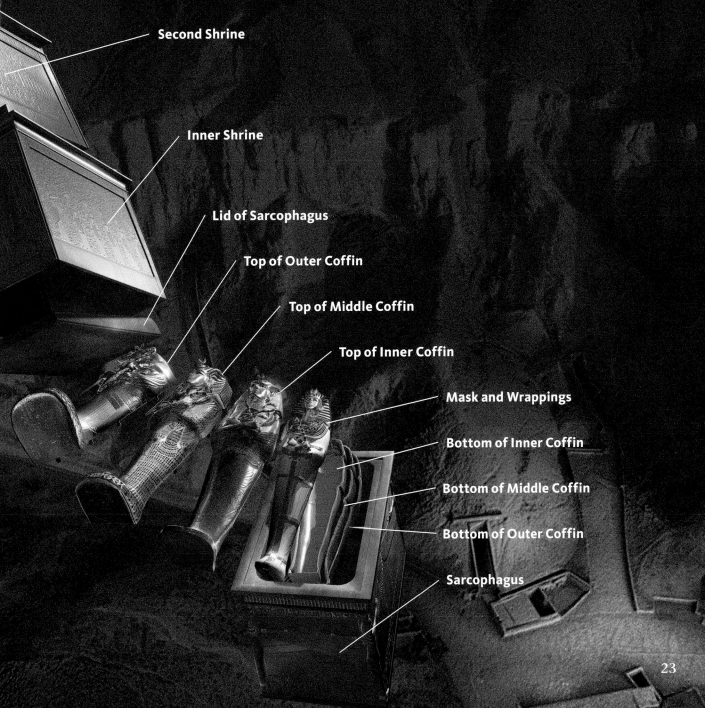

Second Shrine

Inner Shrine

Lid of Sarcophagus

Top of Outer Coffin

Top of Middle Coffin

Top of Inner Coffin

Mask and Wrappings

Bottom of Inner Coffin

Bottom of Middle Coffin

Bottom of Outer Coffin

Sarcophagus

23

The Middle Coffin

FIT FOR A KING

The second of three coffins meant to carry Tutankhamun to the afterlife is called the middle coffin. Measuring six feet seven, it was nestled inside the outer coffin, which measures seven feet three. More elaborately detailed than the outer coffin, the middle coffin held a still more astonishing treasure: the inner coffin, made of pure gold, weighing 243 pounds.

The headdress bears the royal insignia of a white vulture and an Egyptian cobra. These creatures represented the goddesses Nekhbet and Wadjet, who protected the royal family.

The false beard is a common feature found on Egyptian art and sculpture depicting the pharaohs. Here it points upward, identifying the king with Osiris, god of the dead.

Both arms are folded, signifying the King of Egypt. He holds the crook and flail, symbols of royal power. The crook and flail resemble tools used by shepherds and farmers and may symbolize the pharaoh's roles as provider and shepherd of his people.

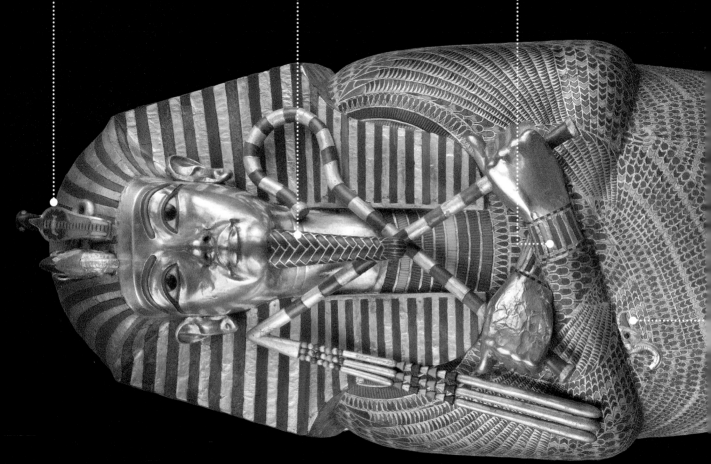

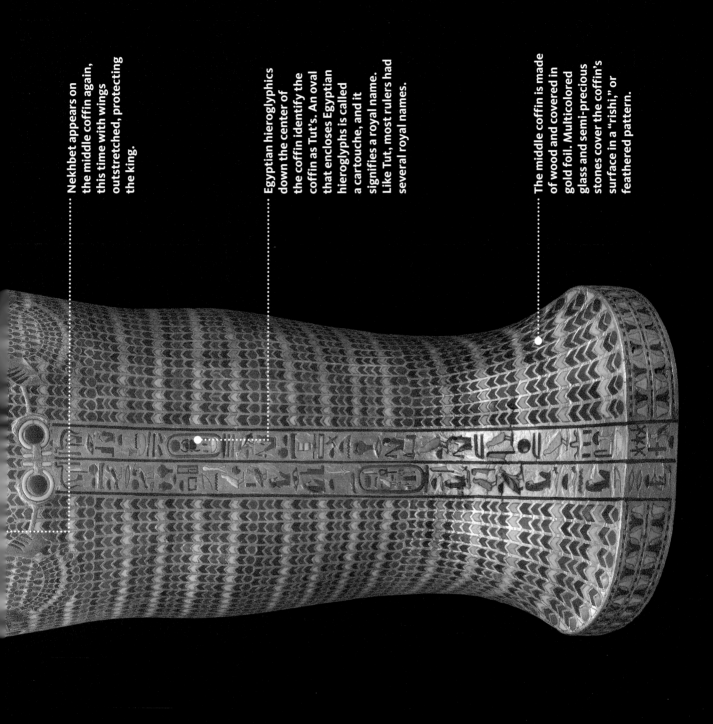

Nekhbet appears on the middle coffin again, this time with wings outstretched, protecting the king.

Egyptian hieroglyphics down the center of the coffin identify the coffin as Tut's. An oval that encloses Egyptian hieroglyphs is called a cartouche, and it signifies a royal name. Like Tut, most rulers had several royal names.

The middle coffin is made of wood and covered in gold foil. Multicolored glass and semi-precious stones cover the coffin's surface in a "rishi," or feathered pattern.

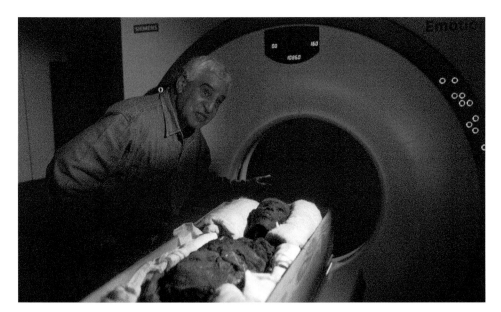

Egyptian archaeologist Zahi Hawass oversees Tut's mummy as it is sent into the portable CT scanner. Computer images of the young king revealed astonishing details.

Analysis would take several weeks to complete—and would reveal no clear evidence for murder. But for now the pressure was off. Sitting back in his chair, Zahi Hawass smiled, clearly relieved that nothing had gone seriously wrong. "I didn't sleep last night, not for a second," he said. "I was so worried. But now I think I will go and sleep."

By the time we left the trailer, descending metal stairs to the sandy ground, the wind had stopped. The winter air lay cold and still, like death itself, in this valley of the departed. Just above the entrance to Tut's tomb stood Orion—the constellation that the ancients knew as the Soul of Osiris, the god of the afterlife—watching over the boy king.

THINK ABOUT IT! |||||||||||||||||||||||||||||||||||||||

1 **Compare and Contrast** What are some similarities and differences between Howard Carter's methods and those of modern archaeologists?

2 **Draw Conclusions** List the possible reasons for King Tut's death named in this article. Which reasons are supported by modern technology?

3 **Analyze Visuals** Choose your favorite image from this article. What does it reveal about King Tut and life in ancient Egypt?

BACKGROUND & VOCABULARY

anatomy *n.* (uh-NA-tuh-mee) a branch of knowledge that deals with the structure of organisms

embalmer *n.* (ehm-BAHL-muhr) a person who treats corpses to preserve them from decay

forensics *n.* (fohr-EHN-ziks) the application of scientific knowledge to legal problems, such as criminal investigations

gilded *adj.* (GIL-duhd) covered with a thin coating of gold

radiology *n.* (ray-dee-AWL-uh-gee) branch of medicine concerned with x-rays or radioactive material

resin *n.* (REH-zin) a sticky substance produced by some plants and trees, usually solid or semi-solid; resins were used in ancient Egypt to prepare mummies for burial.

sarcophagus *n.* (sar-KAHF-uh-guhs) a stone coffin or container to hold a coffin

technician *n.* (tek-NIH-shun) a specialist in the use of a scientific tool or a type of technology

FACE OF A PHARAOH
This forensic reconstruction of
King Tutankhamun is based on
CT scans of his mummy.

Animals
Everlasting

BY A. R. WILLIAMS

Adapted from "Animals Everlasting," by A. R. Williams,
in *National Geographic*, November 2009

Not every ancient Egyptian mummy was a great pharaoh—or even a human. Wrapped in linen and reverently laid to rest, animal mummies hold clues to life and death in ancient Egypt.

An Amazing Discovery

In 1888 an Egyptian farmer digging in the sand near his village uncovered a mass grave. The bodies weren't human. They were feline, ancient cats that had been mummified and buried in pits in huge numbers. "Not one or two here and there," reported the *English Illustrated Magazine*, "but dozens, hundreds, hundreds of thousands, a layer of them . . . ten to twenty cats deep." Some of the linen-wrapped cats still looked presentable. A few even had gilded faces. Village children sold the best mummies to tourists for change. The rest were sold in bulk as fertilizer. One ship hauled about 180,000 mummies to Liverpool to be spread on the fields of England.

In those days generously funded American and European expeditions dredged through acres of desert looking for royal tombs and for splendid gold and painted masks and coffins. The many thousands of mummified animals that turned up were just things to be cleared away to get at the good stuff. Few people studied them or recognized their importance.

In the century since then, archaeology has become more of a science. Workers at archaeological sites now realize the great value that lies in details about ordinary folks: what they did, what they thought, how they prayed. Animal mummies are a big part of that value.

Animal Mummies

"[Animal mummies] are really manifestations of daily life," says Egyptologist Salima Ikram. "Pets, food, death, religion. They cover everything the Egyptians were concerned with." Specializing in zooarchaeology—the study of ancient animal remains—Ikram has helped launch research into the cats and other creatures that were preserved with great skill and care.

As a professor at the American University in Cairo, she adopted the Egyptian Museum's collection of animal mummies as a research project. After taking exact measurements, looking beneath **linen** bandages with x-rays, and cataloging her findings, she created a gallery for the collection. It serves as a bridge between people today and those of long ago. "You look at these animals, and suddenly you say, Oh, King So-and-So had a pet. I have a pet. And instead of being at a distance of 5,000-plus years, the ancient Egyptians become people."

Today the animal mummies are one of the most popular exhibits in the whole treasure-filled museum. Visitors of all ages press in shoulder to shoulder to get a look. Behind glass panels lie cats wrapped in strips of linen that form diamonds, stripes, squares, and crisscrosses. Shrews in boxes of carved limestone. Rams covered with gilt and beads. A gazelle so flattened by mummification that Ikram named it Roadkill. A 17-foot crocodile buried with baby croc mummies in its mouth. Ibises [wading birds] in bundles with intricate decorations. Hawks. Fish. Even tiny beetles and the dung balls they ate.

Some animals were preserved so that the dead would have companionship in eternity.

Ancient Egyptians who could afford it prepared lavish tombs, hoping that everything they assembled would be available to them after death. Beginning in about 2950 B.C., kings of the 1st dynasty were buried at Abydos with dogs, lions, and donkeys. More than 2,500 years later, during the 30th dynasty, a commoner at Abydos was laid to rest with his small dog curled at his feet.

Other mummies were intended to be food for the dead. The best cuts of beef, fat ducks, geese, and pigeons were salted, dried, and wrapped in linen. "**Victual** mummies" is what Ikram calls this gourmet food for the hereafter. "Whether or not you got it regularly in life didn't matter because you got it for eternity."

Connection with Egyptian Gods

Some animals were mummified because they were the living representatives of a god. The city of Memphis, the capital for much of Egypt's ancient history, covered 20 square miles at its largest and had a population of some 250,000. Today the city's crumbled glory lies under the village of Mit Rahina (mit rah-HEE-nah) and its surrounding fields. Along a dusty lane, the ruins of a temple stand half hidden in the grass. This was the mummification house of the Apis bull, one of the most **revered** animals in all of ancient Egypt.

A symbol of strength and manliness, the Apis was closely linked to the all-powerful king. He was part animal, part god and was chosen for worship because of his unusual set of markings. He had a white triangle on his forehead, white winged patterns on his shoulders and rump, the

COSMIC POWERS
This tightly-wrapped linen bundle conceals a mummified falcon. Falcons were revered as creatures with cosmic powers.

outline of a beetle on his tongue, and double hairs at the end of his tail. During his lifetime he was kept in a sacred place, waited on by priests, adorned with gold and jewels, and worshipped by the people. When he died, his divine spirit was believed to move on to another bull. The body of the deceased bull was carried to the temple and laid on a bed of finely carved stone. Mummification took at least 70 days: 40 to dry the enormous amount of flesh, and 30 to wrap it.

On the bull's burial day, people surged into the streets to mourn his death. Wailing and tearing at their hair, they crowded the route to the burial place in the desert. In procession, priests, temple singers, and important officials delivered the mummy to the network of tombs carved into the limestone. There, among the many earlier burials, they placed the mummy in a massive wooden or stone **sarcophagus**. In later centuries, thieves broke into this sacred place. They pried off the sarcophagus lids and stole the mummies' precious ornaments. Sadly, not a single burial of the Apis bull has survived undamaged.

Different sacred animals were worshipped at their own centers: bulls at Armant and Heliopolis (hee-lee-OP-uh-liss), fish at Esna, rams at Elephantine Island, crocodiles at Kom Ombo. Ikram believes the idea of such divine creatures was born at the dawn of Egyptian civilization. At that time heavier rainfall than today made the land green and bountiful. Surrounded by animals, people began to connect them with specific gods according to their habits.

Take crocodiles. Each year they **instinctively** laid their eggs above the expected high-water line of the Nile's annual flood. This annual flood watered and enriched fields and allowed Egypt to be born again year after year. "Crocodiles were magical," Ikram says, "because they had that ability to foretell."

31

GOLDEN COW
A golden mask covers the head of a 4,000-year-old cow mummy. Cow mummies honored Hathor, the goddess of many things, including the sky, women, music, and love.

Sacred Offerings

The news of a good flood, or a bad one, was important to a land of farmers. And so, in time, crocodiles became symbols of Sobek, a water god of fertility. A temple arose at Kom Ombo, one of the places where the swelling flood was first observed every year. In that sacred space near the riverbank, wild crocodiles lay sunning themselves. The Egyptians also kept captive crocodiles that led a pampered life and were buried with due ceremony after death.

The most numerous animal mummies, buried by the millions, were objects offered in prayer during yearly festivals. Like county fairs, these great gatherings enlivened religious centers along the Nile. Egyptians arrived by the hundreds of thousands and set up camp. Music and dancing filled the processional route. Merchants sold food, drink, and souvenirs. Priests became salesmen, offering simply wrapped mummies as well as more elaborate ones for people who could spend more—or thought they should. With incense swirling all around, the faithful delivered their **votive** mummies to the temple.

Some places were connected with just one god and its symbolic animal. But old sites such as Abydos have yielded many kinds of votive mummies. Each is a link to a particular god. At Abydos, **excavations** have uncovered ibis mummies likely representing Thoth (TOHT), the god of wisdom and writing. Falcons probably evoked the sky-god Horus, protector of the living king. And dogs had ties to the jackal-headed Anubis, the guardian of the dead. By donating one of these mummies to the temple, an Egyptian could win favor with its god. "The creature was always whispering in the god's ear, saying, 'Here he is, here comes your devotee, be nice,'" explains Ikram.

Beginning in about 664 B.C., votive mummies became wildly popular. The country had just defeated its foreign rulers, and Egyptians were relieved to return to their own traditions. The mummy business boomed, employing a large number of specialized workers. Animals had to be bred, cared for, killed, and mummified. Materials used in mummifying had to be imported, wrappings prepared, tombs dug.

Despite the religious purpose of the product, **corruption** crept into the process, and sometimes a buyer ended up with a fake. Ikram's x-rays have revealed a variety of rip-offs: a cheaper animal substituted for a rarer, more expensive one; bones or feathers instead of a whole animal; beautiful wrappings around nothing but mud. The more attractive the package, Ikram has discovered, the greater the chance of a fake.

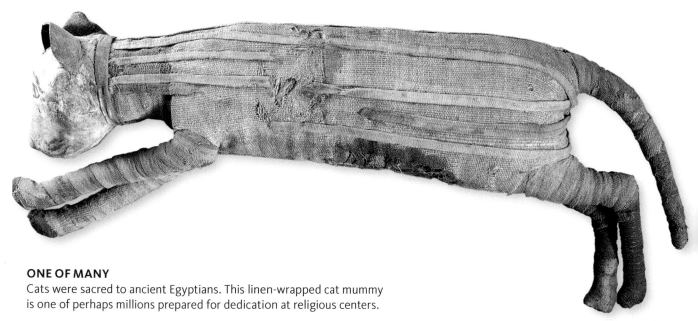

ONE OF MANY
Cats were sacred to ancient Egyptians. This linen-wrapped cat mummy is one of perhaps millions prepared for dedication at religious centers.

AN ANIMAL GRAVEYARD
At Tuna-el-Gebel, archaeologists found an underground complex in which thousands of sacred animal mummies had been entombed, including the baboon shown here.

Studying Animal Mummies

To find out how the ancient mummy creators worked, Ikram conducts experiments in mummification. For supplies she visits the narrow, crooked streets of Cairo's old marketplace. At a small shop just a block from the busy souvenir stands she buys natron, a salt that absorbs moisture and fat and was the key drying agent used in mummification by ancient Egyptian embalmers. Natron is still mined just southwest of the Nile Delta and is usually used for washing. At a shop around the corner, Ikram finds oils that will make dry, stiff bodies flexible again and lumps of incense that will seal bandages when melted.

Her mummifications began with rabbits. They're a manageable size, and she could get them at the butcher. "Instead of making them stew bunnies, I gave them life for eternity," she says. Ikram names all her mummies. Flopsy was buried whole in natron. The body didn't last two days. Gases built up, and it exploded. Thumper had better luck. His lungs, liver, stomach, and intestines were snipped out. He was then stuffed with natron and buried in more of the same. This one survived.

Fluffy, the next candidate, helped explain an archaeological puzzle. The natron packed inside her absorbed so much fluid that it became goopy, smelly, and disgusting. Ikram dug out the mess and replaced it with fresh natron tied in linen bags. These were simple to remove once they got soggy, explaining why similar bundles turn up among ancient mummifying supplies.

Peter Cottontail's treatment was entirely different. Instead of having his internal organs removed, he was injected with a mixture of turpentine and cedar-oil. He was then placed in natron. A famous Greek historian had written about the procedure in the fifth century B.C., but scholars didn't believe him. Ikram's experiment proved him right. All Peter's organs dissolved except the heart, the one organ ancient Egyptians always left in place.

Like the animals mummified more than 3,000 years ago, Ikram's animal mummies went to a happy afterlife. Once the lab work was done, she and her students wrapped each body in bandages printed with magical spells. Saying prayers and burning incense, they laid the mummies to rest in a classroom cabinet, where they draw visitors—including me. As an offering, I sketch plump carrots and symbols to multiply the bunch by a thousand. Ikram assures me that the pictures have become real in the hereafter, and her rabbits are twitching their noses with joy.

THINK ABOUT IT! |||||||||||||||||||||||||||||||||||||

1 **Find Main Ideas and Details** List reasons why the ancient Egyptians created animal mummies.

2 **Compare and Contrast** Compare and contrast the way animal mummies were treated in ancient Egypt, in the late 19th century, and in Ikram's modern lab.

3 **Evaluate** Describe Ikram's work with animal mummies. Why has her work been important?

BACKGROUND & VOCABULARY

corruption *n.* (kor-UHP-shun) a departure from what is honest or correct

excavation *n.* (ex-kuh-VAY-shun) the act or process of digging to uncover buried items

instinctively *adv.* (in-STEENK-tiv-lee) prompted by natural reactions; without thinking

linen *n.* (LIHN-uhn) cloth made from flax; a plant that grows in Egypt

revere *v.* (ruh-VEER) to show devotion and honor to

sarcophagus *n.* (sar-KAHF-uh-guhs) a stone coffin

victual *n.* (VIH-tuhl) food usable by humans

votive *adj.* (VOH-tiv) offered as a prayer

EXPLORER'S JOURNAL

with **Sarah Parcak**

WITH COUNTLESS ANCIENT CITIES AND PYRAMIDS STILL BURIED BELOW EGYPT'S ENDLESS SAND, WHERE DO YOU POINT YOUR SHOVEL?

Sarah Parcak is an archaeologist who relies on **satellites** in space to answer this very question. Orbiting hundreds of miles overhead, satellites provide important information, including television and phone signals. Satellites can also use powerful space cameras and other tools to locate structures less than two feet wide and completely invisible to the naked eye.

Sarah Parcak is an **Egyptologist** and a National Geographic Fellow. She is also a leader in the young field of satellite archaeology. She uses futuristic tools to unlock secrets from the past and transform the way discoveries are made. "We're using satellites to help map and model . . . features that could never be seen on the ground," she explains. Satellites are locating features that

WHAT THE CAMERA SEES
Sarah Parcak uses satellite photos to reveal archaeological details that until now have escaped human eyes.

me three and a half years. . . . Less than one percent of ancient Egypt has been discovered. . . . Why not use the most advanced tools we have to map . . . and protect our past?"

Ancient Egyptians built with mud bricks. These bricks hold water and are denser than surrounding soil. Satellites can detect those differences in density. When viewed from hundreds of miles up, the differences can help reveal outlines of buried cities, temples, tombs, and roads.

Parcak stresses that these exciting moments happen only after careful research and study in the lab. "We don't just grab an image, flip it into the computer, and press a button. I've spent more than 10,000 hours of my life staring at satellite imagery to understand what I'm seeing."

In fact, she feels her most important contribution isn't discovering ancient sites. Parcak has also written the first book on using satellite archaeology. This work will allow the next generation of students to learn and advance the new field.

Parcak looks forward to using data from the new technology to answer some of archaeology's biggest questions. For instance, why did Egypt's great pyramid age end? By revealing thousands of new sites, satellite maps show trends and population shifts. Scientists can relate these to other important facts such as global climate events. For example, scientists know there was a global **drought** around the time people stopped building pyramids. Parcak believes the sudden halt in pyramid building was caused by this climate event. People were forced to move from the sites of the pyramids to big cities where the Nile still flowed strongly.

"To me, these are the . . . questions technology can help answer," she says. Parcak hopes her work will help people understand patterns of human behavior over time. Studying the past may help explain how humans succeed or fail during times of hardship or change. "How did we shape the landscape, and how did the landscape shape us?" she asks.

Parcek is amazed at the rate technology is improving. "It's getting much better, much faster. [Satellite] images will soon portray objects less than one foot in size."

have been covered by soil, forests, or modern buildings for centuries.

Parcak uses advanced computer programs, satellite images—and old-fashioned digging. With these tools, she has identified thousands of new sites. Lost pyramids, temples, homes, and even entire towns are among her finds.

"The time and cost savings to the field of archaeology are enormous," Parcak reports. "Before doing fieldwork in Middle Egypt, I analyzed satellite imagery to determine exactly where I wanted to go. Within three weeks I found about 70 sites. If I had approached this as a traditional foot survey, it would have taken

As a child Parcak remembers peering through a stereoscope, then state-of-the-art technology used by her grandfather, a well-known pioneer of **aerial** photography in forestry. That experience inspired Parcak to take a course in space archaeology during her last university semester. "One course can change your life," she tells her own students today.

"This isn't just another 'gee whiz' toy," she says. "It's a genuine scientific tool with proven, published results. It has so much potential and possibility. It transforms every aspect about how we see and understand our past."

Satellite Archaeology

Sarah Parcak and her high-tech tools are adding tremendously to the historical record of ancient Egypt. Archaeology is a messy business. Digging holes—in the dirt, in the sand, and in the rain forest—is essential. However, using satellite archaeology, Parcak is pioneering a new way to search, with no shovels needed.

Like medical scans that let doctors examine parts of the body they couldn't otherwise see, satellite images help scientists find and map long-lost rivers, roads, and cities, and discern archaeological features in conflict zones too dangerous to visit. "There is much we miss on the ground," emphasizes Sarah Parcak.

Through thousands of hours of trial and error Parcak has perceived what the human eye can't. Hard-won successes have taught her what works: combining and processing images so she can peer into the **infrared** part of the light spectrum, which is invisible to the naked eye. The images allow her to detect subtle surface changes caused by objects like mud bricks a foot or less underground.

In 2011, relying on infrared satellite pictures, Parcak and her team identified 17 potential buried pyramids, some 3,000 settlements, and 1,000 tombs across Egypt. At the 3,000-year-old city of Tanis, once a thriving and powerful capital in the Nile Delta, she found evidence of hundreds of dwellings. "Above ground, you can't see anything," she says. "It's a silty mound with brown, muddy earth covering everything." After a few days of processing and peering at the images, "this amazing map popped out," she recalls. (See the visual at right.)

Using laborious, low-tech excavation, it might have taken a century to assemble a similar city plan. But old-fashioned digging is exactly what's needed to confirm these high-tech finds. A French team has made a start, excavating a single Tanis house. When it comes to archaeology, distance provides crucial perspective, but there's no substitute for being up close.

....

Adapted from Hannah Bloch, "Satellite Archaeology," *National Geographic*, February 2013, pp. 60–61.

THINK ABOUT IT! |||||||||||||||||||||||||||||||||

1 Summarize How is technology changing the practice of archaeology?

2 Pose and Answer Questions What questions would you like to ask Sarah Parcak about satellite archaeology or about her career?

3 Identify Problems and Solutions What problems does satellite archaeology solve for researchers?

BACKGROUND & VOCABULARY

aerial *adj.* (AYR-ee-uhl) in or from the sky

drought *n.* (DROWT) a long period without rain

Egyptologist *n.* (ee-jihp-TAW-luh-jihst) a researcher who studies ancient Egypt

infrared *adj.* (in-fruh-REHD) light with a longer wavelength than what is visible to the naked eye

satellite *n.* (SAT-uh-lyte) a machine launched into space that orbits Earth or another body for the purposes of collecting information or for communication

Peering into Egypt: The City of Tanis

Tanis, Seen From Space ∨
A computer program combines two satellite images into a high-resolution picture that reveals subtle changes in the landscape caused by buried features—in this case, houses.

At the Surface ∨
To the naked eye, there is no clue of what lies beneath the top layer of sand and soil. The site of Tanis looks like a muddy mound.

Mapped Out ∨
After hours of study by scientists such as Sarah Parcak, the satellite images reveal hundreds of houses in the vicinity of a temple.

Temple

Early small homes

Medium and small homes

Large homes

Large homes

Ramses
the Great

BY RICK GORE

Adapted from "Ramses the Great," by Rick Gore,
in *National Geographic*, April 1991

Ramses II reigned for more than 60 years, fathering at least 90 children and bringing prosperity and peace to the Egyptian empire. He built more colossal structures and had his name carved on more stone surfaces than any other pharaoh. He was Egypt's "King of Kings" during its splendid golden age. Today, his name has come to symbolize the grandeur and the great monuments of ancient Egypt.

The Young Ramses

In 1295 B.C., the Egyptian crown passed to a commoner who had risen through the **bureaucracy** to the rank of vizier, the second most important post in the realm. This was Pramesse, Ramses' grandfather, who began a new **dynasty** as Ramses I. He ruled for a brief 16 months before his son Seti, a vigorous warrior, assumed the crown.

Ramses was about eight when his father became pharaoh. Seti must have filled his son with romantic tales of war. It is easy to imagine him personally showing the boy how to charge a chariot into battle. Seti also infused Ramses with his own two great dreams: to reclaim the lands lost to the Hittites (HIH-tytes), Egypt's enemies to the northeast, and to build colossal monuments in the style of the great kings of earlier dynasties.

Seti began making annual **incursions** into Hittite territory. He probably did not permit his son to go into battle for a few years. However, he did name Ramses commander in chief of the army at age ten. At about 14, Ramses was allowed to join his father on the battlefield. Together Seti and Ramses swore to recapture from the Hittites the city of Kadesh, which guarded the trade routes to the east. They took the city briefly, but it fell back to Hittite rule as soon as they returned to Egypt.

Meanwhile, Seti had other plans for Ramses. Pharaohs took multiple wives, and Seti selected several for his son and heir. The message was clear: have children. Ramses wasted no time. His principal wife, the lovely Nefertari (neh-fuhr-TAR-ee), quickly produced a son. His second favorite wife, the clever Istnofret, soon delivered another. Ramses' other wives produced still more royal children.

During this period Ramses spent much time overseeing his father's building projects. An age of massive construction had begun a century before by pharaohs worried about the power of bureaucrats and military leaders. The pharaohs of this era began to emphasize the ancient belief that they were gods and to build statues and temples on a grand scale to reaffirm that message. Seti and Ramses may not have been merely glorifying themselves with their constructions, but meeting a job requirement.

The **divinity** of the pharaoh was emphasized in Thebes, the country's religious capital and the site of the temples of Karnak and Luxor—sacred complexes where pharoahs competed to overshadow their predecessors' monuments. We can only imagine how Seti felt when he arrived at Karnak for the first time as pharaoh. Once a commoner, he was now divine, entitled to enter the temple's inner **sanctum**, the "holy of holies" where the god Amun lived.

On their first official visit to Karnak both father and son saw how the temple had been defaced. Even the name and figure of Amun had been chiseled off its monumental walls. Seti sat down with the priests to plan new walls and an impressive hall of columns that today still dwarf human visitors. The hall itself is 56,000-square-feet, and the columns soar to nearly 70 feet. On both sides stand forests of 61 smaller columns, each 42 feet high. Covering the surrounding walls are painted carvings detailing great moments in the lives of Seti and Ramses.

The walls of Karnak still provide revealing glimpses of how a pharaoh was supposed to feel. "His Majesty," reads one inscription, "exults at beginning the battle. He delights to enter into it. His heart is gratified at the sight of blood."

TEMPLE ON THE WATER
In the 1960s, the construction of the Aswan High Dam threatened to submerge Abu Simbel. The Egyptian government dismantled the temple and moved it to higher ground. Today, Abu Simbel looks over Lake Nasser, the lake created by the dam.

Ramses the King

When Seti died at about age 50, Ramses, still in his 20s, became king. Among his first duties was to sail again to Thebes that September, to participate in the festival of Opet. At this festival a pharaoh performed perhaps his most important religious function.

The Opet festival came at the time of the year when, according to religious belief, the god Amun was dying, and the world was threatened with chaos. Each year, amid singing, dancing, and celebration, the pharaoh and the priests of Amun led a procession that carried a golden statue of the dying god from Karnak's inner sanctum to a waiting barge. This barge was then towed behind the royal barge to the temple at Luxor. While the high officials ceremonially rowed the royal barge

upriver, soldiers and peasants on the shore with towlines did most of the work.

At Luxor, the statue of Amun was escorted into the temple, where it stayed for about two weeks while undergoing secret ceremonies of renewal. The pharaoh led those rituals, which simultaneously renewed his own *ka*, or divine spirit. The rites also reaffirmed his **legitimacy** as ruler and mediator between the gods and humans. So in year one of his reign, Ramses saved the world from chaos for the first of many, many times.

Ramses next sailed north on his golden barge to the sacred city of Abydos, the home of Osiris, god of the afterlife. Seti had been building a spectacular

temple there. Ramses was shocked to find it unfinished. "A son should be concerned to care about his father," he declared. He ordered an intensified building program and then proceeded to put his own name and image in many places in his father's temple.

Ramses completed his own temple at Abydos. He built a great city in the Nile Delta, calling it Pi-Ramses, House of Ramses. He finished the columned hall at Karnak and commissioned other temples in nearly every important Egyptian city. He also took credit for many structures built by earlier pharaohs, removing their names and substituting his. He installed a colossal statue of

IN YEAR ONE OF HIS REIGN, RAMSES SAVED THE WORLD FROM CHAOS FOR THE FIRST OF MANY, MANY TIMES.

LARGER THAN LIFE
Two enormous statues of Ramses seated on thrones guard the entrance of the Luxor Temple. As in life, Ramses remains an imposing figure.

himself and commanded workers to carve his name in stone.

In the fifth year of his reign, Ramses decided to retake the strategic city of Kadesh. With an army of 20,000 soldiers, he marched northeast. His move provoked a dramatic showdown with the powerful king of the Hittites.

> "IF RAMSES HAD LOST THE BATTLE OF KADESH, YOU WOULD NEVER HAVE HEARD OF HIM."

"If Ramses had lost the Battle of Kadesh, you would never have heard of him," says Kenneth Kitchen, the world's leading expert on Ramses. "He would have been an obscure king who ruled four and a half years." And lose it he almost did. The Hittite king had amassed an army of 40,000 men. Poor Egyptian patrolling allowed Hittite chariots to catch Ramses' main force off guard. The Egyptian troops scattered in panic. Ramses found

himself abandoned. Nevertheless he leaped into his chariot, telling his trembling shield bearer: "I shall go for them like the pounce of a falcon, killing, slaughtering, and felling them to the ground."

Is this an accurate account? We don't know. We have only Ramses' version of the events. He says that he fought alone, charging six times back into the fray. Then suddenly the luck of Amun blessed him. Egyptian reinforcements arrived. The Hittites were thrown into confusion. The Hittite king was suddenly watching his soldiers fleeing before the wild young pharaoh, leaping into the river and swimming for safety behind their own lines. The next day brought reality to both sides. Neither army was likely to displace the other. So Ramses declared a great victory and led his battered army home.

Later Years

By the time Ramses reached his mid-40s, he had given up his annual campaigns against the Hittites, but not his mania for building. Shortly after returning from Kadesh, he had begun planning his grandest monument—Abu Simbel.

He chose a remote site far to the south, where bluffs of pink sandstone towered above the Nile. He had four 67-foot seated statues of himself carved into the rock. Then, behind the statues, his workers cut a temple 160 feet deep into the hillside. They adorned the walls with the glories of Kadesh. On a nearby bluff he built a second monument for his favorite wife, Nefertari.

Ramses' feelings for his principal wife are evident in the beautiful companion statues of Nefertari. For her, he found words of unusual tenderness. "Possessor of charm, sweetness, and love," he had inscribed in her tomb.

It is tempting to compare Nefertari with Ramses' other chief wife, Istnofret. Little is known of her, but Kitchen speculates: "Nefertari had the looks. He was obviously proud of her, showing her off all the time. But I think Istnofret had the brains. It's her offspring that wielded the most power as Ramses aged." And one of her sons eventually inherited the throne. Istnofret also outlived Nefertari, who disappears from official papers after Ramses' 21st year in power. At that time the Egyptians and the Hittites had finally signed a long-lasting peace treaty, and Nefertari wrote a cordial letter to the Hittite queen.

Nefertari was probably still alive at the dedication of her great monument at Abu Simbel, but she may have been ill. Her daughter is the one depicted at the ceremonies. Nefertari may have been resting on the royal barge, too fatigued to play her role after the long, difficult journey.

How did Ramses die? Probably of old age. His mummification and burial rites likely took the traditional 70 days.

Within 150 years of Ramses' burial, thieves robbed his tomb and **desecrated** his mummy. Twice reburied by priests, the body long kept its secrets. In time, though, X-rays revealed that Ramses suffered badly from arthritis in the hip, which would have forced him to stoop. His teeth were severely worn, and he had dental infections and gum disease.

Was Ramses pompous, cruel, and self-centered? By our standards, certainly. He left no evidence of human complexity or bitterly learned lessons. But he did love deeply. And he surely experienced human suffering. Did he really believe he was a god? Who can say? But clearly, he strove to be the king his country expected—providing wealth and security—and succeeded. He also wanted to live forever. More than most, this man got what he wanted.

THINK ABOUT IT! |||||||||||||||||||||||||||||||||

1 **Sequence Events** List the main events in Ramses' long life.

2 **Form and Support Opinions** Which qualities and achievements do you think are most responsible for Ramses being called "the great"? Explain your answer.

3 **Synthesize** At the end of the article, the author writes, "[Ramses] also wanted to live forever. More than most, this man got what he wanted." What does the author mean?

BACKGROUND & VOCABULARY

bureaucracy *n.* (byoo-RAH-krah see) a large group or several layers of government officials

desecrate *v.* (DEH-seh-krayt) to damage an item that is holy or historically important, such as a monument or grave

divinity *n.* (duh-VIN-ih-tee) the state of being a god

dynasty *n.* (DY-nuh-stee) a series of rulers from the same family

incursion *n.* (un-KUR-juhn) military invasion

legitimacy *n.* (luh-JIH-tuh-muh-see) the quality or fact of ruling by hereditary right

sanctum *n.* (SAYNK-tuhm) a sacred, or holy, place

Document-Based Question

The ancient Egyptians can seem impossibly distant and exotic. They lived so long ago, and their beliefs were so different from ours. Even after more than a century of research and study, many mysteries about the ancient Egyptians remain. With each discovery, however, more information about life in ancient Egypt comes to light. The picture that is emerging is sometimes surprisingly familiar.

DOCUMENT 1 Primary Source

Advice from a Teacher

In ancient Egypt, a scribe's job was to record information such as legal contracts, court proceedings, wills, medical procedures, and quantities of grain harvested. Egypt's government and society relied on the work of scribes. An inscription from Memphis gives this advice from a teacher:

> Be a scribe! It saves you from toil and protects you from all kinds of work. It spares you from using hoe and [farm tools], that you need not carry a basket. It keeps you from wielding the oar and spares you torment, so that you are not subject to many masters and endless bosses. . . . No the scribe, he directs all the work in this land.

from "Ramses the Great," *National Geographic*, April 1991

CONSTRUCTED RESPONSE

1. What does this inscription tell you about the position of a scribe in ancient Egyptian society?

Statue of Egyptian scribe

DOCUMENT 2 Primary Source

Finding King Tut

In 1922, Howard Carter discovered the tomb of Tutankhamun. It was the most complete pharaoh's burial ever found, filled with a wealth of treasures and valuable information about ancient Egypt. After weeks of studying and preserving items found in the tomb's outer chambers, Carter at last unsealed the burial chamber and beheld the pharaoh's coffin.

> [W]hen, after about ten minutes' work, I had made a hole large enough to enable me to do so, I inserted [a flashlight]. An astonishing sight its light revealed, for there, within a yard of the doorway, stretching as far as one could see and blocking the entrance to the chamber, stood what to all appearances was a solid wall of gold. . . .
>
> It was, beyond any question, the [burial] chamber in which we stood, for there, towering above us, was one of the great [gold-covered] shrines beneath which kings were laid. So enormous was this structure . . . that it filled within a little the entire area of the chamber, a space of some two feet only separating it from the walls on all four sides.

from *The Complete Tutankhamun: The King, the Tomb, the Royal Treasure* by Nicholas Reeves. Thames and Hudson, Ltd., London, 1990

CONSTRUCTED RESPONSE

2. How do you visualize Tut's burial chamber? What can you infer about the ancient Egyptians' attitude toward the pharaohs and their burials?

How was life in
ancient Egypt
like life today?

DOCUMENT 3 Artifact

Tomb Painting

This painting from the tomb of Mennah at Thebes shows a grain harvest. The bending figures are workers placing grain in bags. The seated figure is an official who counts the bags. The rest of the figures in the painting are scribes recording the number of grain sacks on sheets of papyrus.

CONSTRUCTED RESPONSE

3. What modern jobs would you compare to the ones you see in this painting?

PUT IT TOGETHER

Review Think about your responses to the question following each document and what you have learned about life in ancient Egypt.

Compare and Contrast Sketch a two-column chart or a Venn diagram. Use it to note similarities and differences between life in ancient Egypt and life in modern times.

Write How was life in ancient Egypt like life today? Write a paragraph that compares life in these two time periods, focusing either on the similarities or on the differences.

INDEX

||||||||||||||||||||||||||||||||||||||||||||||||||||||

SKILLS